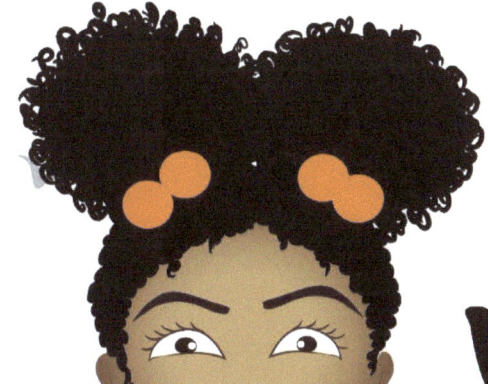

Love My Kinks Coils & Waves

Written & Illustrated by Kimeca Caine

I Love My Kinks Coils & Waves

By Kimeca Caine

Copyright © 2020 by Kimeca Caine
All rights reserved. This book or any portion thereof
may not be reproduced or used in any manner whatsoever
without the express written permission of the publisher
except for the use of brief quotations in a book review.
Printed in the United States of America

First Printing, 2020

Self Published, Kimeca Caine, Creative Roots Design Studio LLC

ISBN: 9798605959076

This is to all of the little girls with curly, kinky or wavy hair:
Your hair is beautiful just the way it is and so are you.

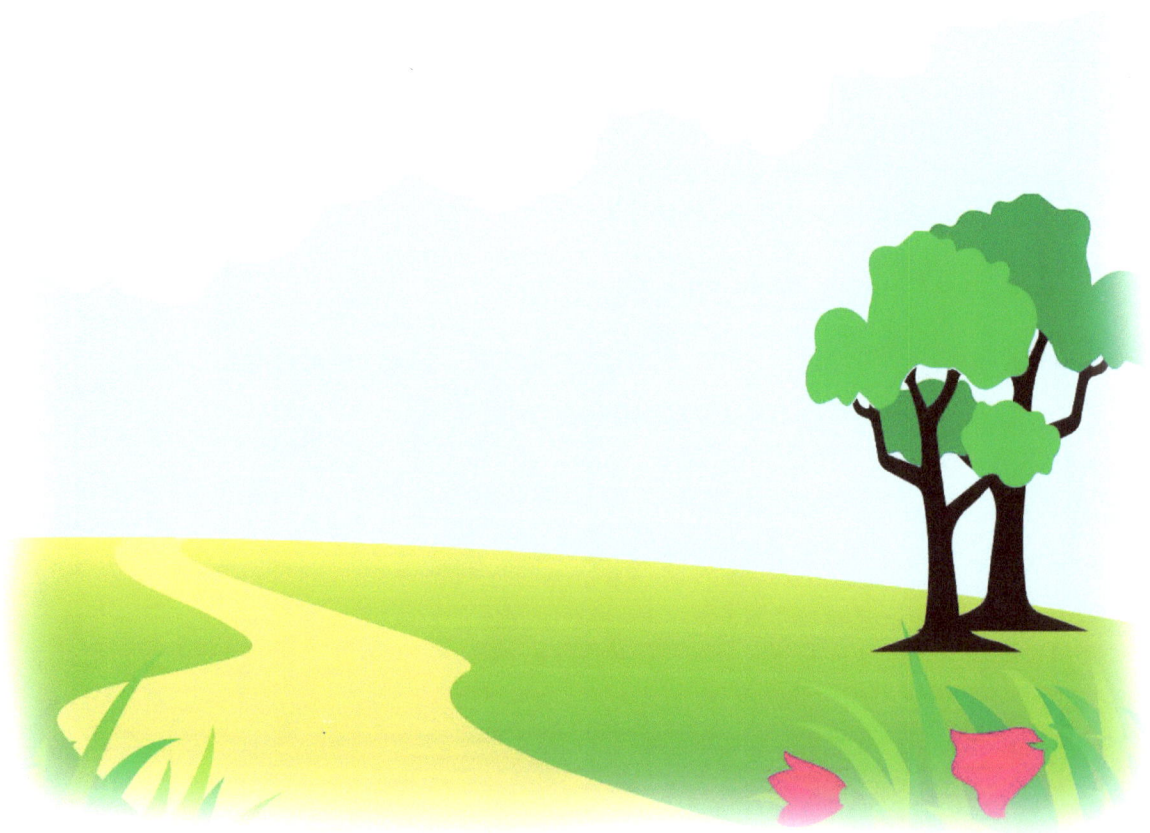

Dedication

I would not have been able to make this book possible
without my mother Fay Thompson and my son Jaydin Griffith.
In addition I would like to thank my family, friends and clients for the
inspiration and motivation to bring this project to fruition.
Thank you all.

I love my hair!

My hair is a part of me.
With lots of care, my kinks,
coils, and waves will grow
healthy and strong, making it oh
so big, fluffy and fun!

My hair is BOLD!

I love my kinks coils and waves!

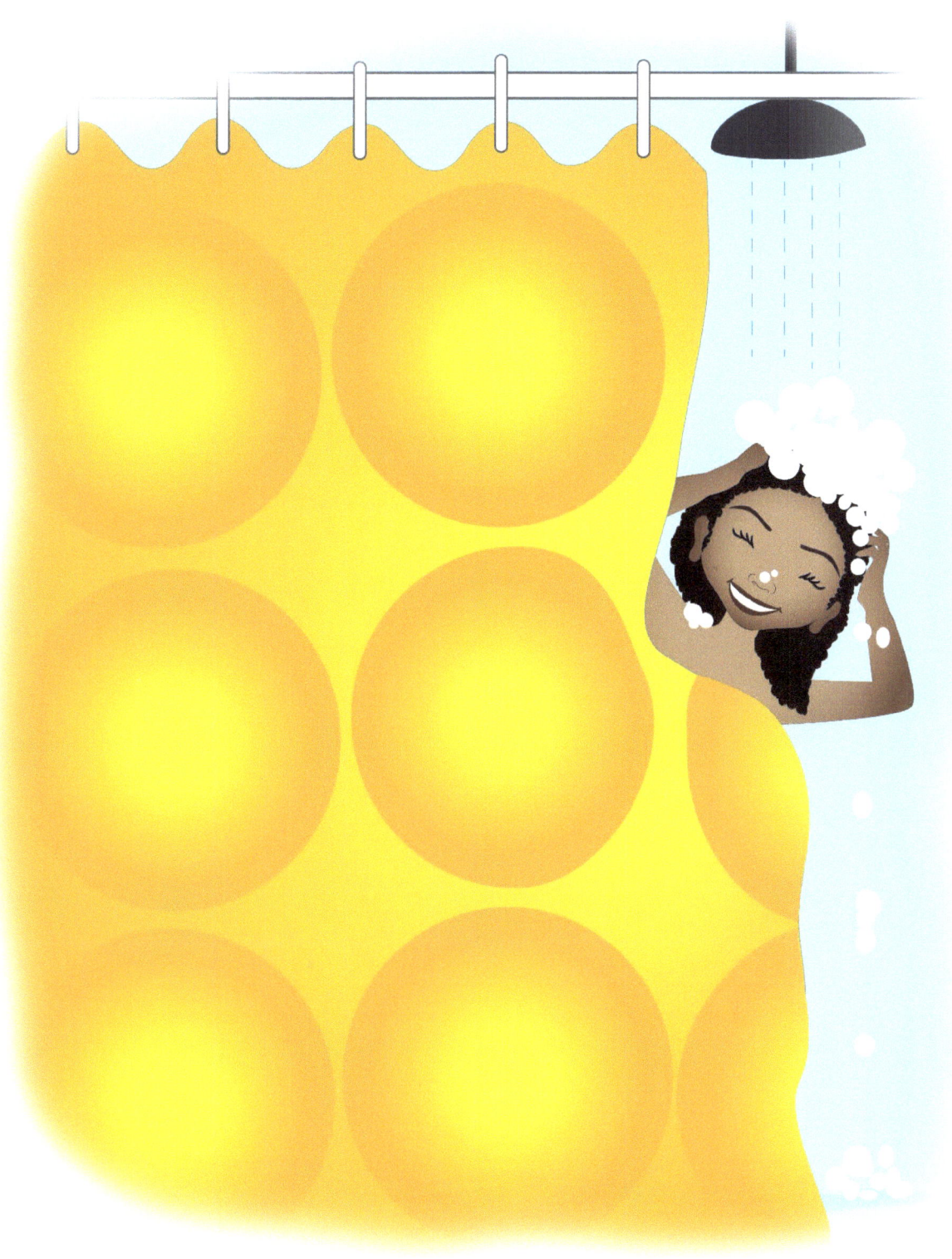

I love my hair!

My hair stands up and out,
like a crown on my head.
Just like the kings and queens
in a book that I just read.

My hair gets a little tangled
when dry but I don't worry.
Mommy uses Kim's Coil Oil,
so when my hair is being combed
it can be done in a hurry.

I am resourceful!

I love my kinks coils and waves!

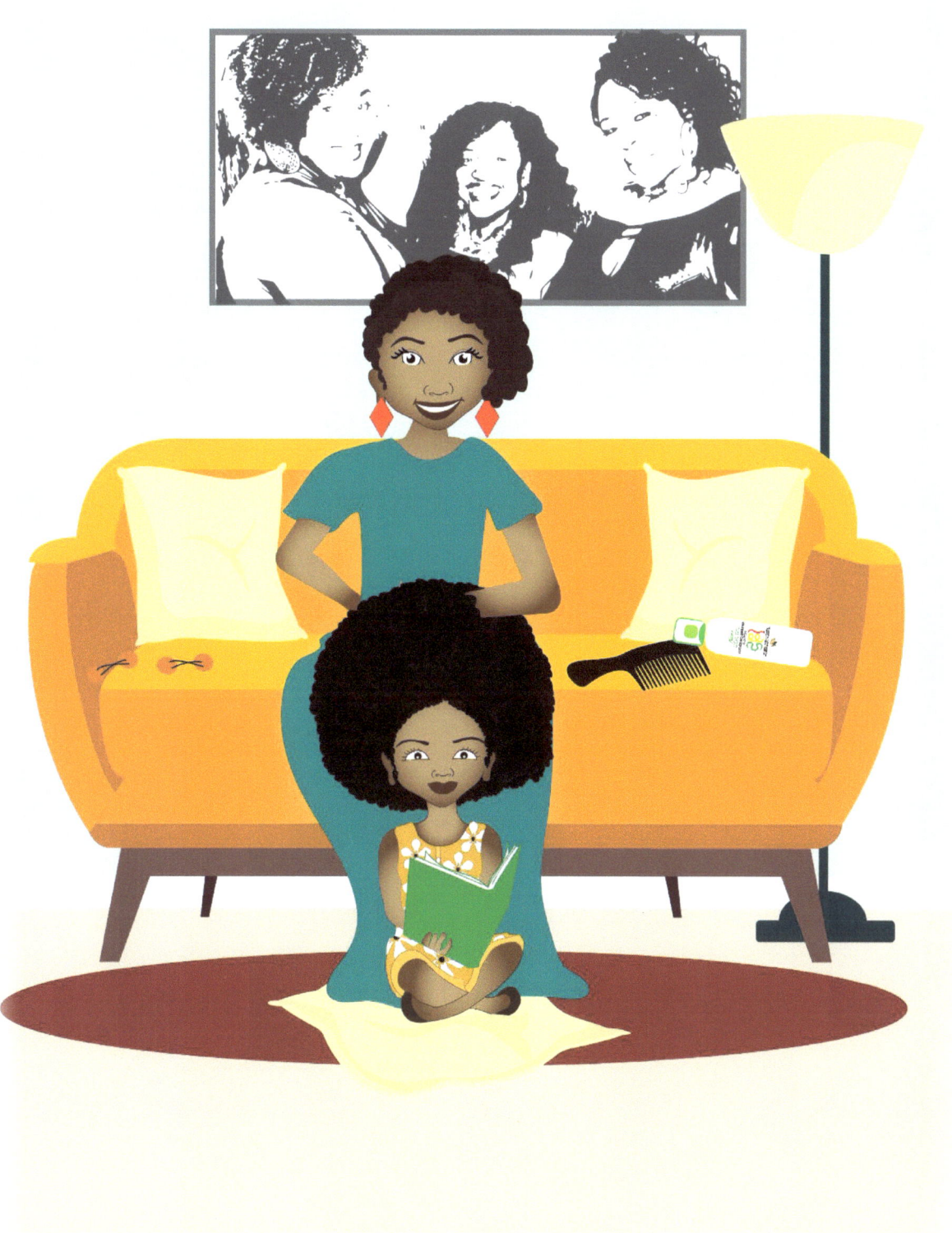

I love my hair!

Sometime mommy takes me to Ms. Kim.
She is a Hair Stylist who gives me a trim.

The hair salon is a fun place to be,
There is so much there to see.

I watch hair of all color, texture and length being done.
The Hair Salon is truly fun!.

I can sit patiently to get my hair done!

I love my kinks coils and waves!

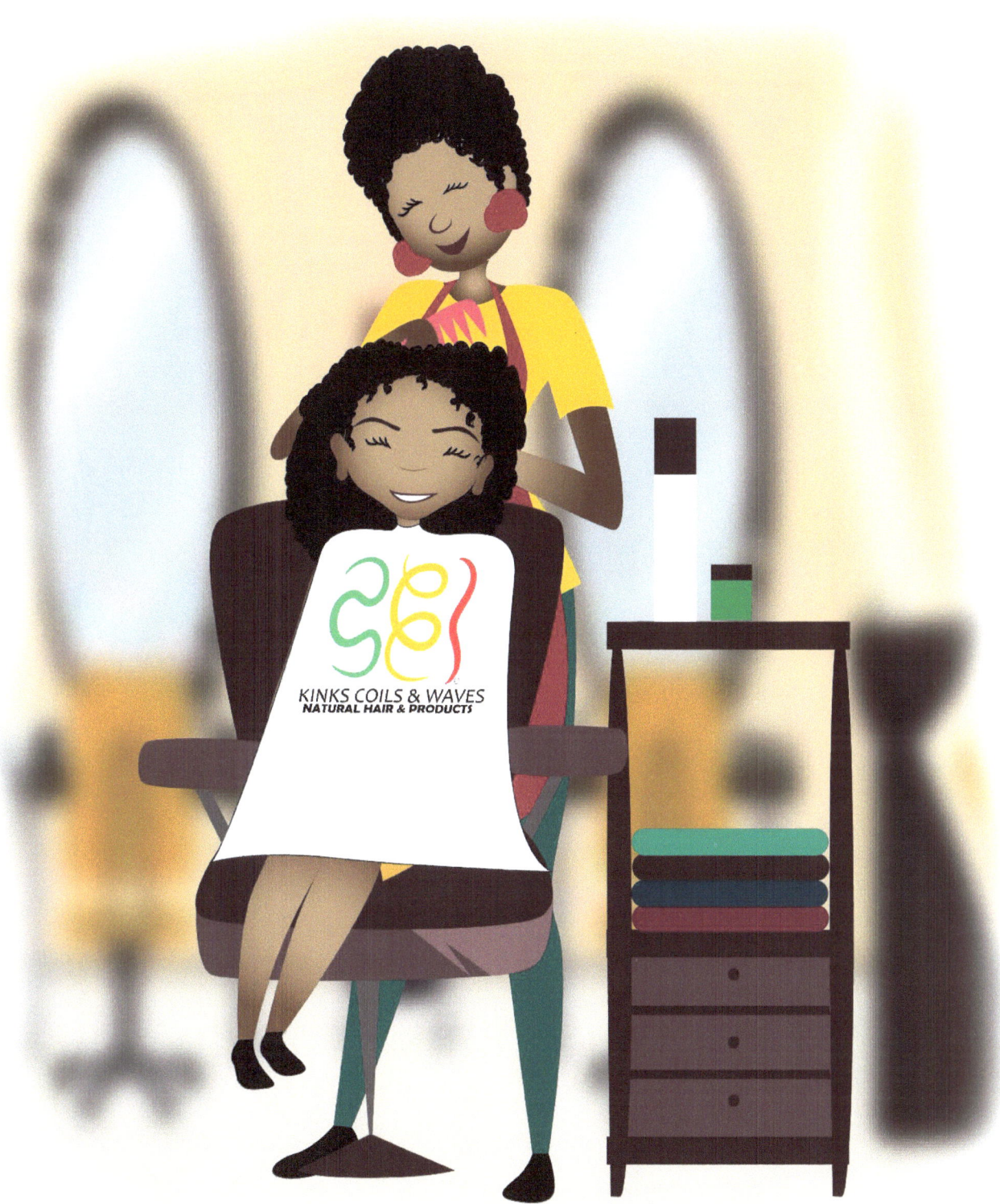

I love my hair!

You would be surprised to see,
just how magical my hair can be.

It looks long and sleek when blow dried or pressed,
and when water touches it again,
my curls come right back
because my curls are the best!

I am magical!

I love my kinks coils and waves!

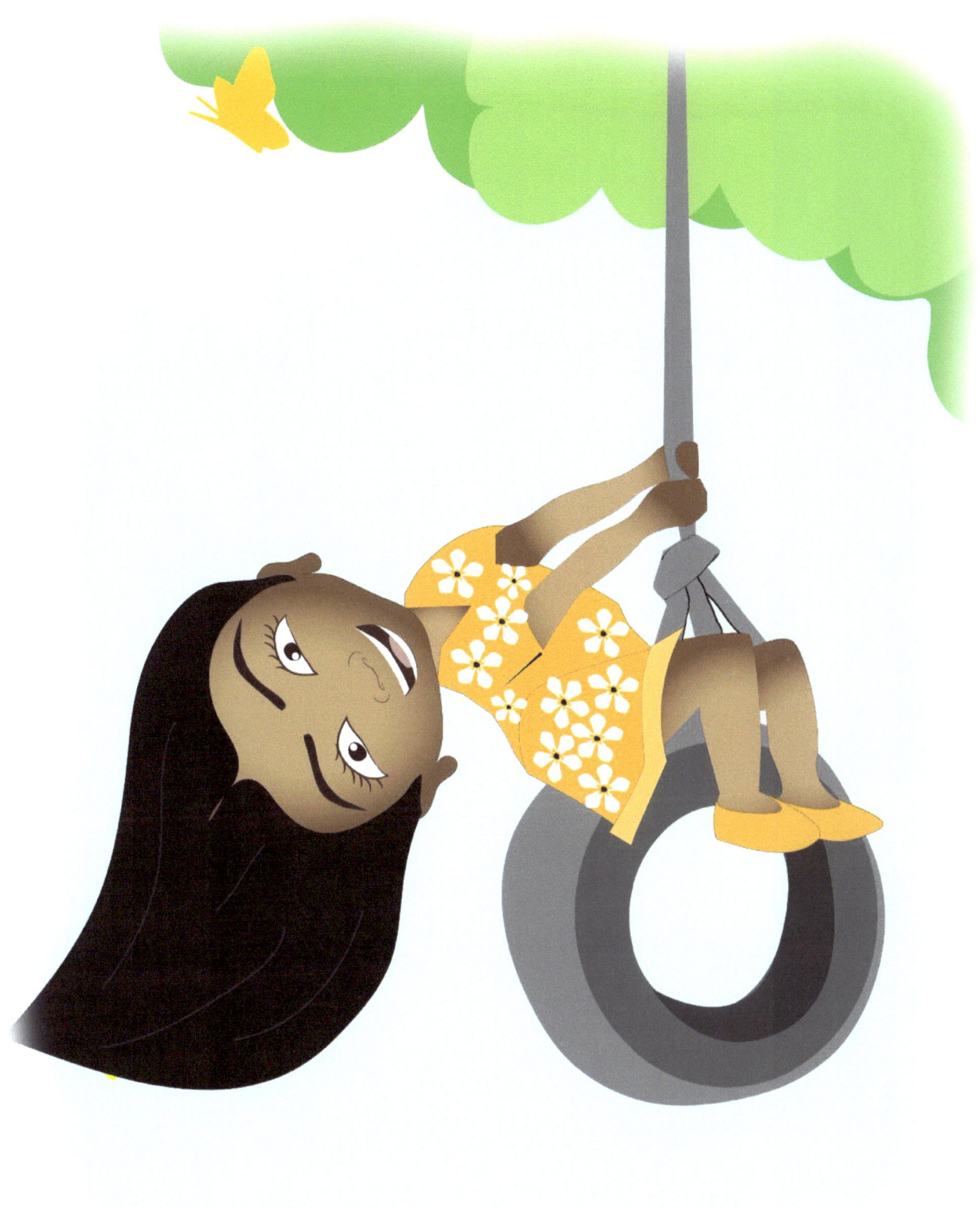

I love my hair!

My hair can be styled in so many ways
I have a different hair style for all the days.

Buns, bantu knots, braids
twists, beads and bows,
and sometimes even corn rows.

I am a trend setter!

I love my kinks coils and waves!

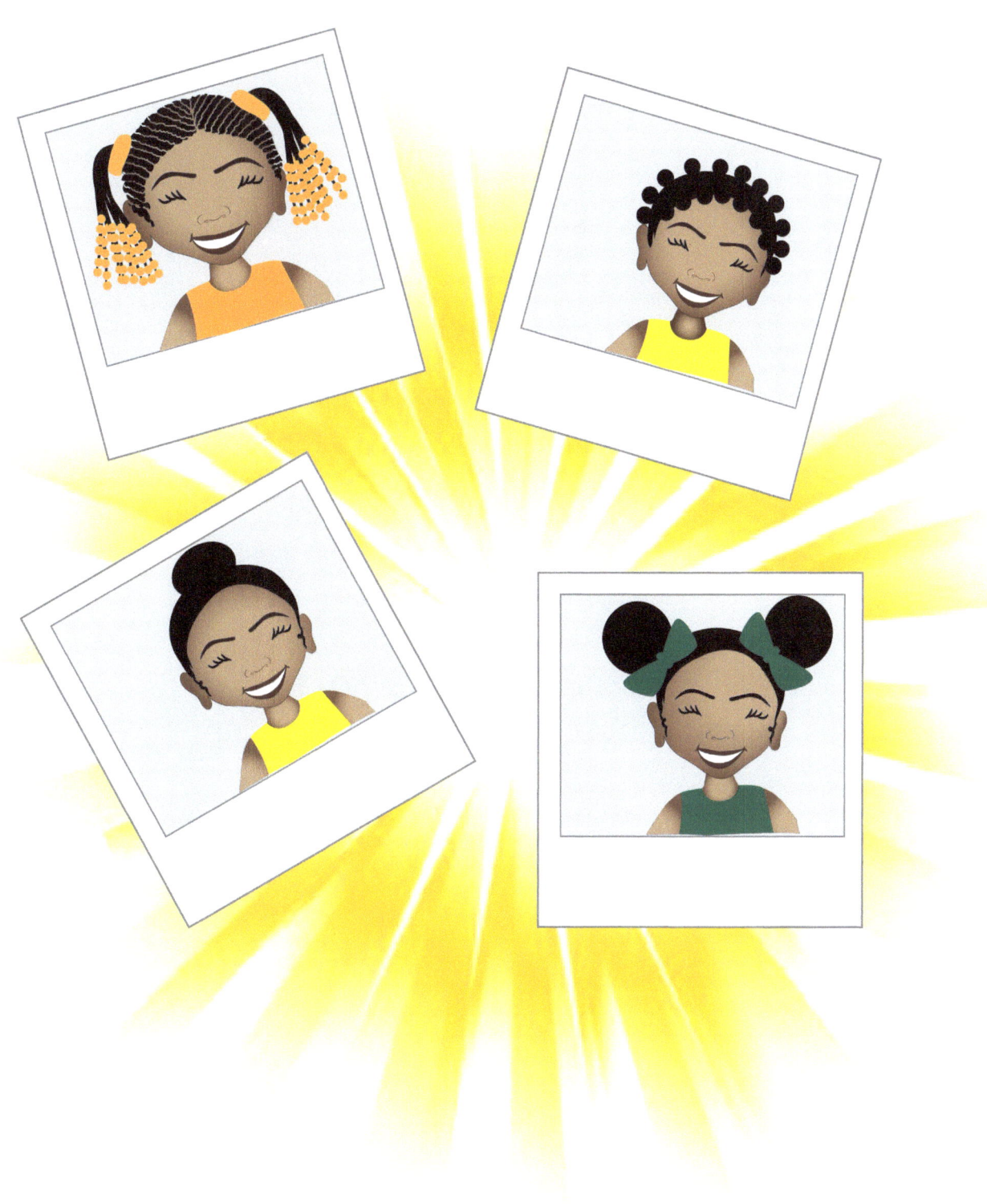

I love my hair!

My hair sometimes has a mind of its' own.
If I don't detangle it for a long time locs
will form, they are naturally grown.

My natural curls would intertwine,
making thick strands as strong as a vine.

My Hair is versatile!

I love my kinks coils and waves!

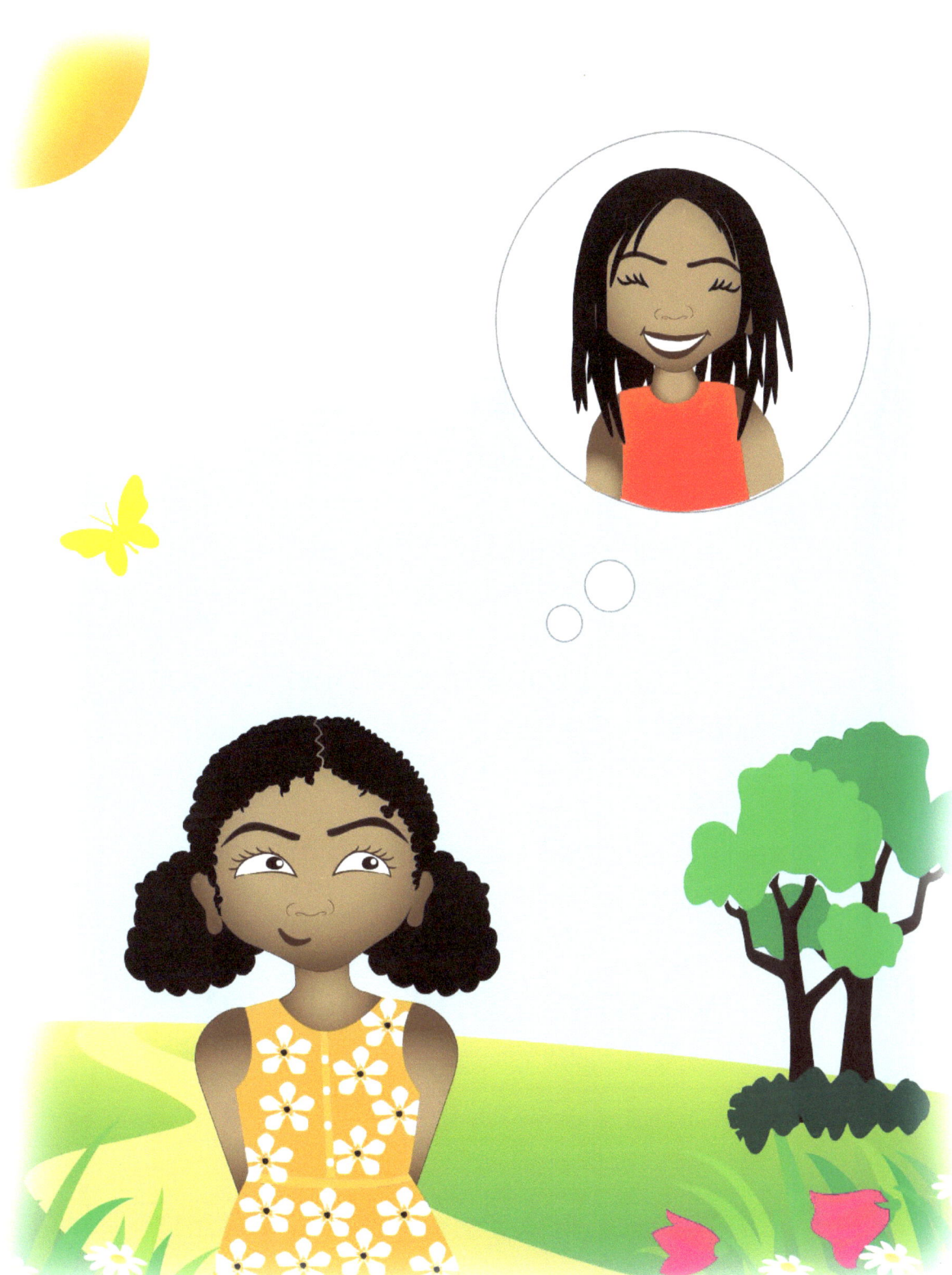

I love my hair!

So I take care of hair you see!
I want my hair to be the best it can be.

I shampoo my hair, and deep condition it as well.
Let's not forget I drink lots of water, and eat fruits
and vegetables that the markets sell.

A healthy body will produce healthy hair!

I love my kinks coils and waves!

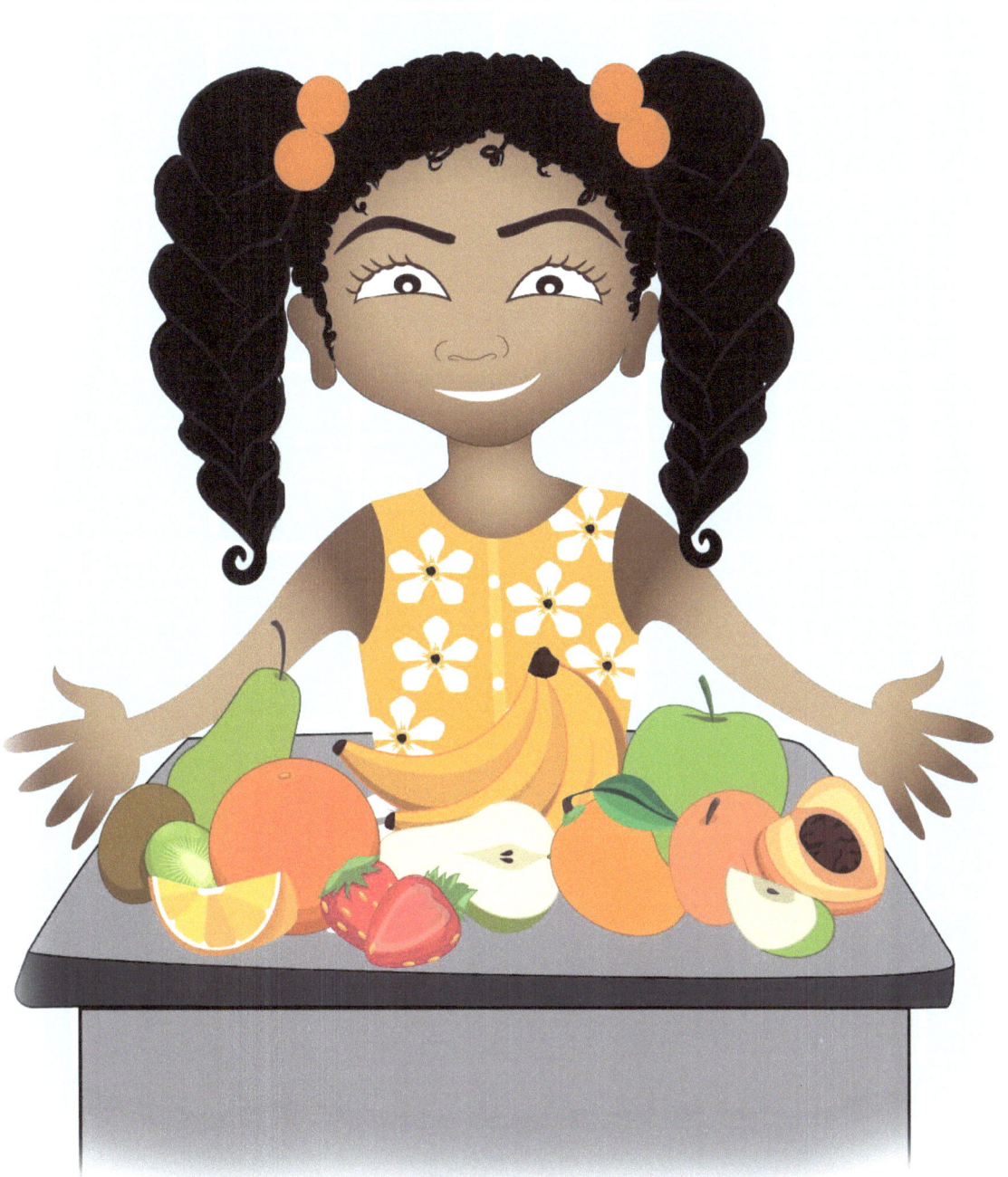

I love my hair!

I love my coils, they are bouncy and round.
But on my head so many
different textures can be found.

My hair spirals in ringlets big and small,
that are twisty kinky and soft when
on my shoulders they fall .

I am so unique!

I love my kinks coils and waves!

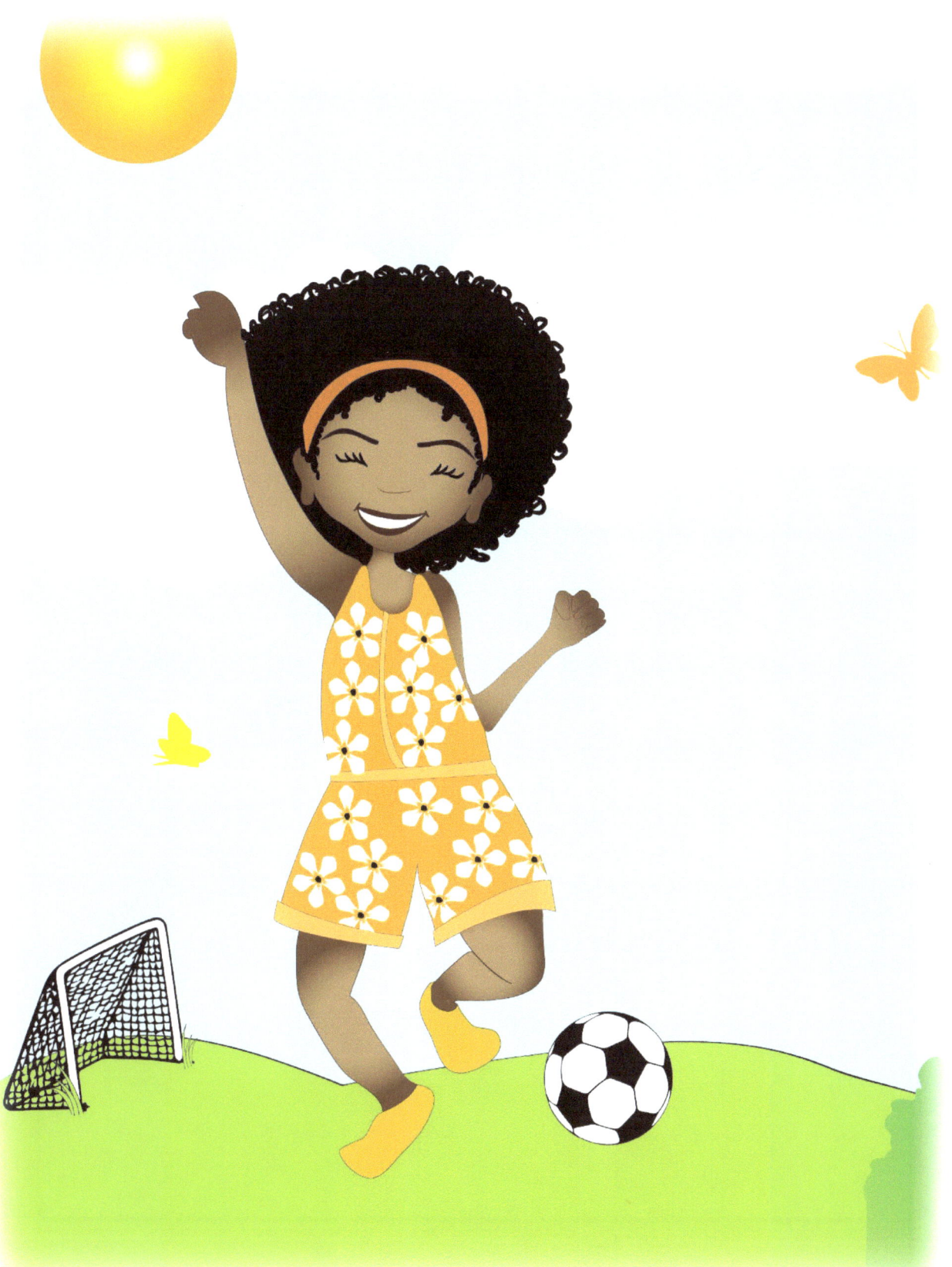

I love my hair!

My hair will grow and so will I.
We will both become stronger with time.

With love, patience and care,
I'll learn so much more about myself and my hair,
but no worries I'll be sure to share.

I love me,
I love my hair,

I love my kinks coils and waves!

How about YOU!?

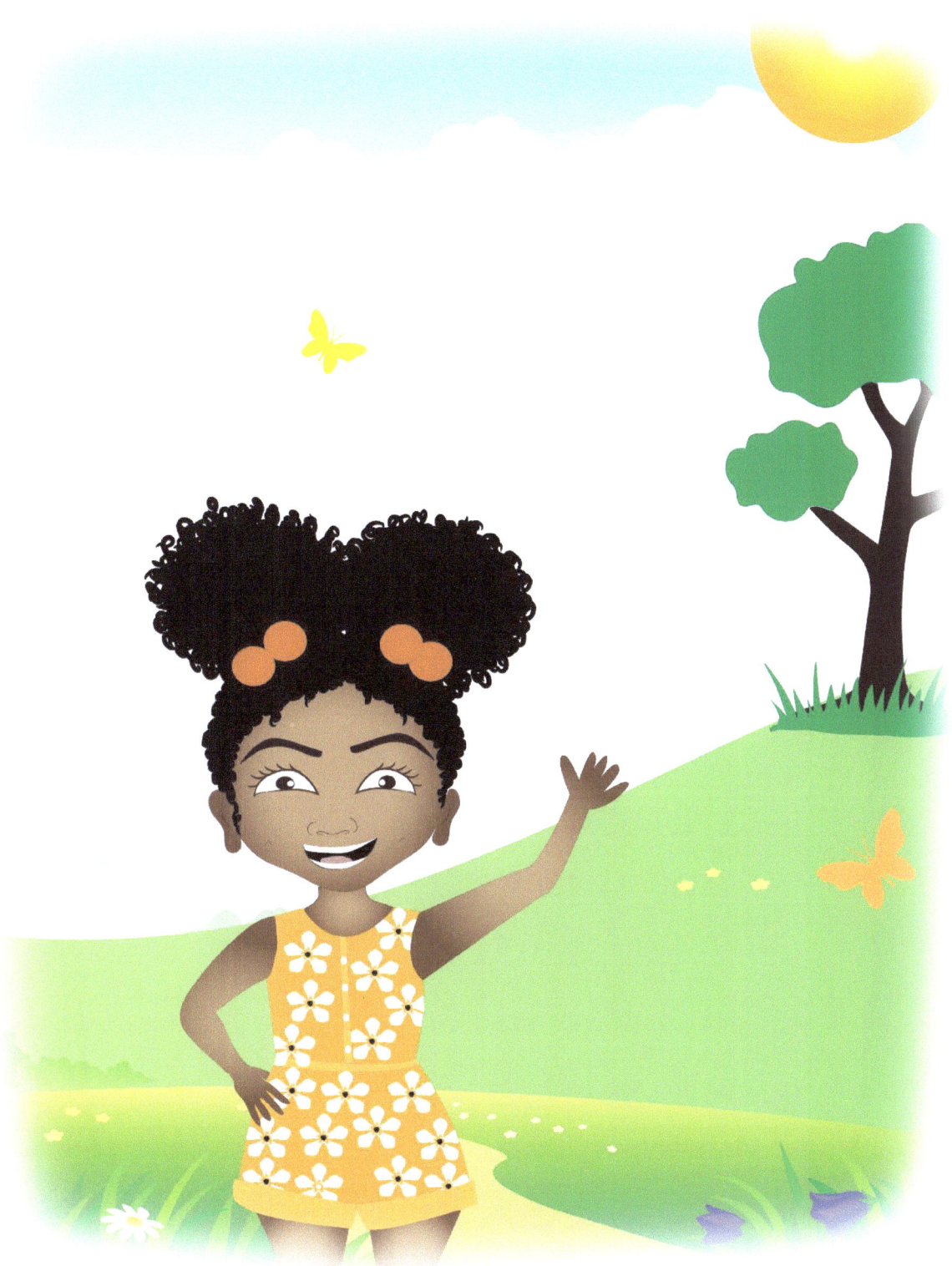

Kinks Coils Waves Word Search

Word List

BRAIDS
BRUSH
COCONUT
COILS
COMB
CURLS
FRUITS
HAIR
HAPPY
JUMP
KINKY
OIL
PLAY
SHORT
TWISTOUT
VEGETABLES
WALK
WATER
WAVE

```
W D C S C F S R S K G B A Y H
A U O L R O C L L H L J A A W
T E J U M O C A I B O B S L S
E O I X M E W O Q O E R A P L
R T I B B N R B N X C S T B Q
S H Z L Z V L T C U E M I O P
B H S U R B L M G L T J X D R
R D L K I N K Y B T F Y S M K
A M R I A H P A G J P W A V E
I E U C E K T S N P W Y V L T
D N C O A E S R A C L O C I P
S X V X G Z N H V P O B L A P
O S D E N F M C J T M T Q R D
D F V T W I S T O U T U B W H W
D W V S J I O M I X U J I J
```

What do you love about you?

1. _____
2. _____
3. _____
4. _____
5. _____
6. _____
7. _____
8. _____
9. _____
10. _____
12. _____
13. _____
14. _____
15. _____
16. _____
17. _____
18. _____
19. _____
20. _____
21. _____
22. _____
23. _____
24. _____
25. _____
26. _____
27. _____
28. _____
29. _____
30. _____
31. _____
32. _____
33. _____
34. _____
35. _____
36. _____
37. _____

COLOR ME

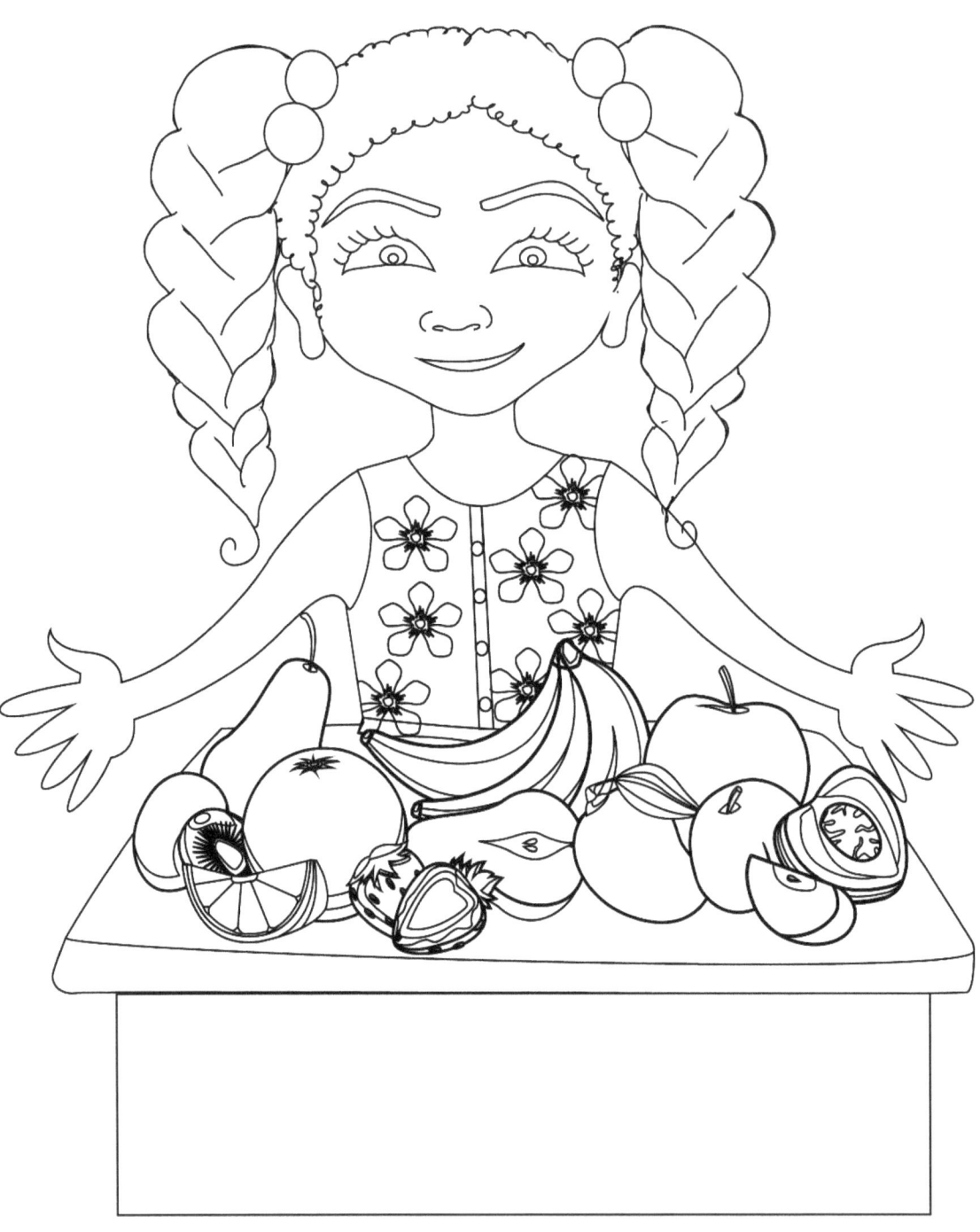

> Look in the mirror and repeat these words as often as you can, say them loud and proud!

I am STRONG
I am KIND
I am UNIQUE
I am SMART
I am RESPECTFUL
I am MAGICAL
I am INNOVATIVE
I am TRUSTWORTHY
I am POWERFUL
I am BRAVE
I am HELPFUL
I am a LEADER
I am TALENTED
I am FUN
I am LOVED

www.ingramcontent.com/pod-product-compliance
Lightning Source LLC
Chambersburg PA
CBHW051830210526
45473CB00005B/1809